EMBRACING THE PRESENT

EMBRACING THE PRESENT

AURORA WINTERS

CONTENTS

1 Introduction   1

2 Understanding the Concept of Now   3

3 Benefits of Living in the Present Moment   5

4 Practical Techniques for Being Present   9

5 Overcoming Common Obstacles to Being Present   13

6 Incorporating Mindfulness into Daily Life   17

7 The Neuroscience of Mindfulness   19

8 Mindfulness in Different Cultures and Traditions   21

9 The Intersection of Mindfulness and Psychology   25

10 Mindfulness in the Workplace   29

11 Mindfulness for Children and Adolescents   31

12 The Role of Mindfulness in Health and Wellness   35

13 Ethical Considerations in Mindfulness Practice   39

14 The Future of Mindfulness Research and Application   43

15 Conclusion   47

CHAPTER 1

Introduction

Many of us live our lives plagued by worry, regret, and dissatisfaction. The year 2020 has shown us many shortcomings in virtually all the components of our lives - with family, profession, living situation, social life, etc. Living in the past can only bring our thoughts around decay, loss, and nostalgia for what once was. Living in the future draws upon what hasn't quite happened, feeding on anxiety and worry. Much of our tension can be in these times that have passed or have yet to happen. The option is in the present moment - to live now. In "The Power of Now: A Guide to Spiritual Enlightenment," Eckhart Tolle explores the skill of living in the now.

Utilizing simple language and an easy question and answer format, Tolle offers insight into his spiritual experience - which forever changed his personal experience. His knowledge connects the awareness of now and provides armor against lives that are ruled by thoughts, feelings, and concepts. By connecting the space between thinking and thought, one can learn objectivity, inner peace, and altered mind clarity while managing the intersection of profession, career, individual style, individual attitude in worldly customs. By focusing on appreciating the space in between moments and breath, we can live a happy, fulfilling life - a life guided by faith and presence.

Background and Importance of Living in the Present Moment

The future is indeed extremely important. It is through our work and our behavior today that we prepare our social and emotional contexts of tomorrow. Society's strong push to overcome our objectives makes the future dominate our actions, thoughts, and attitudes. The investment which is made for future living leaves a very intense mark and it is logical that the worries about our future have an impact on our lives. But our life can only effectively be invested in the present; afterward, nothing will remain except our memories. We can only accumulate moments and experiences through our journey, fully lived with the awareness that we are dedicating our time to us. It is becoming increasingly difficult to find moments of great meaning in our present time due to our endless number of preoccupations with the future. Now, we lead a poor life full of activity and experiences. We ought to remember that interest in taking interest in the present lives involves laying the foundations of our future as well as lead a life that is both balanced and healthier.

Ours is a fast world; everyone and everything seems to be moving at an incredible pace. The outburst of technological advances has turned our lives into a surrounding that alters direction each and every single day. This constant change is making a deep impact on the human being, as most individuals are experiencing lives full of tension and anxiety in a frenetic world, which often leaves us with the sensation that there is not enough time to carry out our daily tasks. The future is a preoccupation that demands all our attention and, due to this, we are a generation of very worried people. In many of our minds there often lies that essential doubt: is the investment in our well-being, which should be given to the present, as efficient as the one invested in the future's concerns? The answer should be a resounding no. We are effectively worried about the future, but the most important thing is being done right now.

CHAPTER 2

Understanding the Concept of Now

"Clock time is not just making an appointment or planning an activity" - Eckhart Tolle. We have created time to measure and quantify the reality of the physical world. However, the construction of our mind is the only reality where time is present and created to such a great extent. The past and future are illusions. They do not exist and always seem to be drawn by the mind. Although we need the mind to navigate through life, it is essential that we never let the mind possess our whole existence where the present doesn't exist at all. The power of Now is the gateway to inner transformation. It has the ability to change our mindset, heal painful thoughts, and make us truly understand the reality around us. Not until we begin to think of time as always living in the present will we truly emancipate our thoughts and live life as it is truly meant to be lived.

The concept of 'now' has rarely been so vividly conceptualized as in Eckhart Tolle's "The Power of Now," where he moves the reader beyond the concept of time as linear and a never-ending present. He meshes the importance of living in the present moment and talks about the necessity for humankind to shed our collective mindset of future-driven thinking. This is in order to move away from a state of increasing mass-emotional dysfunction towards one of deeper and lasting fulfillment and inner peace. "The Power of Now" shows us the way. This essay highlights the major insights mentioned in this remarkable piece of work.

Defining the Present Moment

The present is a concept that is flawed with the impossible mission of creating a sense of isolation from past and future. The desire to achieve such isolation discourages any study of the present, but the fact that the present is the only thing we have cannot be changed. The attention span that we have in the present is our limiting factor. We are prisoners of our next moment, of our earthly lives, in the chain of time. It is the present that we have to know how to handle. The main work that details how to make the most of the increasing opening of consciousness is not a new practice or concept. It was the discovery of established contemplation, meditation. Periodic intervals of contemplation devote awareness to the present.

We use the word "present" not only when we speak of the moment that has just passed, which will soon be gone, but also when we speak of something very particular, right in front of us, something very concrete. Both interpretations very ably illustrate the sense of "present moment." The present is not a specific amount of time; rather, it is our awareness of any widening, of our attention throughout our entire lives. The degree of opening our range of vision is the difference between we becoming aware of our true nature or remaining in our current of illusion.

CHAPTER 3

Benefits of Living in the Present Moment

When you accomplish this, life will become more enjoyable for you to experience, which will then allow much more to be celebrated. Your mind will be free to focus on the task at hand, and this can make routine chores a lot more pleasant. Another significant benefit of living in the present moment is that it makes you appreciate life more. You'll find beauty in things you usually overlooked because your focus was directed towards something that wasn't happening right now. You can see other people's faces, truly appreciate what they look like in the shining sun. You can enjoy the activities for what they are, rather than looking to get them done as soon as possible so that you can move on to the next task. Life's great moments will pass you by if you don't pay special attention to them. You don't want to wake up each day with the regret of not having fully lived your life, by focusing on all the 'problems' you were experiencing at that particular time. Become attentive and wake up to the overwhelming beauty and possibilities life has to offer.

There are several practical benefits to living in the moment. First of all, if you concentrate more on the present, you will notice that fewer thoughts of remorse and guilt will fill your mind. Don't waste your time regretting things which took place in the past, and don't dread what's coming up in the future. It's understandable that you need to perform certain tasks ahead of time, but these should only be plans you take care of when the time comes. What I learned after a while - and what was much more beneficial - is that all the stress and pressure which came with these tasks were not of any use. The amount of nervousness and anticipation of completion could get really high causing a lot of pain, and this was not only for me, but also for the people around me. Instead, if you live in the moment and take care of your responsibilities when it's time, you will perform them at your best, without much stress. It's always better to find pleasure in your work, rather than rushing through it.

Mental and Emotional Well-being

Current worries: If someone is a talented professional, is committed to attending meetings about a problem, and engages work partners to develop potential solutions, they can discern an acceptable course of action. If a friend has gone into a city to go shopping and promised to return in three hours but is late for several reasons, you can think of ways to help her on your own initiative. If your child, partner, friend, or parent suffers from illness, you can learn how to help. The difference between now and the past is that the present cannot be revisited. No one can change anything about the present by acting in the past or wishing they had acted differently. Since the body and mind are completely bound to the current emotional reaction, the negative influence of the past is numbed by concentrating on the hearing, rainfall, and air temperature. When thinking of something pleasant, minds are peaceful, joyful, beautiful, and kind.

Mental and emotional well-being. Living in the present has a powerful effect on our mental and emotional well-being. We often respond to stressful experiences such as a troubled relationship, financial concerns, or a backlog of tasks to complete with a sense that these problems are insurmountable. Over time, contemplation of these concerns often leads to feelings of inadequacy, helplessness, hopelessness, and depression. But if we clear our minds of everything but the present, we can feel happy and peaceful at any time. Meditation and most relaxation techniques promote this mental shift by encouraging people to take charge of their thought processes and focus on building connections in the mind and body. This power gives them the strength to stay in the present for as long as they wish. They can then turn to thoughts of the past and future without triggering the negative response.

CHAPTER 4

Practical Techniques for Being Present

1. As it is always the case with this type of technique, it is essential to remember that both good and bad thoughts should not be suppressed. This only reinforces the idea of "I" - the false self. The acceptance of bad thoughts will lead to their weakening. The technique of reverse ideation will also help with negative thinking. When you make up your mind to do one thing, you must put aside all other thoughts. Practicing this simple method will make you look at the present moment, at any present moment with a fresh eye. This form of surrender is a pleasure, not a sacrifice. Once I surrendered, I realized that no matter what was going to happen, everything was going to be fine. As long as you are communicating, you should act without doubt as to the scope of the possibilities.

2. There is another simple, effective technique for observing thoughts and, at the same time, freeing oneself from the ego - meditation on bodily sensations. In this case, you need to focus on the various sensations of the body and let the body tell you what it feels. Such a meditation could look like the following: close your eyes. Feel any discomfort or tension - there will always be discomfort or tension somewhere. Focus your attention on the intrinsic feeling of that

area of the body. When the pain disappears from your perception, it means that you have focused your attention, that penetrating light inside you has passed into the area of ultimate wisdom and intelligence - that part of the body. Keep it tight, in an expanded, open, continuously conscious, vibrant and welcoming space. If you wait long enough, the tight, inner feeling of letting go of tension in the specific area you are concentrating on finally lets go. In the meantime, you are completely safe because you have penetrated into the nature of the energies of the life of the body.

Mindfulness Meditation

You can, if you wish, attend classes in mindfulness meditation at hospitals, clinics, or educational centers. Many people learn the principles by themselves, though, by reading relevant books and/or following guided meditations on CDs, such as Jon Kabat-Zinn's Full Catastrophe Living. Before you begin a session, remove any stressful thoughts from your mind. Concentrate first on your breathing patterns. Now pay attention to where your mind is going. If it has slipped sideways to let in some irrelevant, stressful thought, let your breathing bring you back to focusing on the here and now. Gradually, the mind will become more focused, and the time devoted to sessions of mindfulness meditation will increase. Gradually, you may notice that deliberately concentrating on the present moment starts to infiltrate the rest of your life too.

Mindfulness involves paying careful attention to what's happening in the present moment, and often this is achieved more readily if we have a clearer mind. To this end, some people find mindfulness meditation useful. Developed from ancient Buddhist meditation practices, its advocates claim that regular practice can help reduce stress, increase concentration levels, and enable people to live in the present moment. Stripped of all religious or spiritual overtones, mindfulness meditation can help you learn ways of quietening the mind so you can focus more on the moment—a simple but profound idea. It's proven to be a powerful tool for quietening the mind and nurturing the spirit and is very effective at reducing stress and enabling owners to live more in the present moment, but it does take time and dedication to learn.

CHAPTER 5

Overcoming Common Obstacles to Being Present

To annihilate the present, that is to say, to solve a problem, you need to actually reach the state of presence, the present moment. If this seems a paradox, there are certain Darwinian victories that favor predatory behavior - war, for instance - but obvious authoritarian interventions help to eliminate the warrior from its warrior's responsibilities. All of the actions of the predator are entirely valid: the awareness of being present or the testimonial reality of being present fools what is actually a reflex, disengaging most calculators from acting other than in a state of deep internal focus, his eyes fixed upon the ultimate prize. The concept helps manifest you - as predator-watcher, as observer, so previous separatist definitions will still register the face of the wise man shouting, just behind the body that should be in the here and now.

If you are not fully here and now, you are not solving problems. Overcoming common obstacles to being present. You may have noticed that being present - being fully in the here and now - gets a bad press in our global culture. It's much underrated. People everywhere are beginning to realize that they need the here and now: they want to enjoy the fullness of a present moment, urgent as it may be, or simply remaining in a state of watchfulness, with no particular content to attend to. No wonder; without it, problem solving becomes virtually impossible. Or show me the person who has the slightest capacity to solve a problem whose only function is to anticipate future states of anxiety, to call them timid, inappropriate, anxious, emotional, and so on.

Dealing with Distractions

The most important factor in handling distractions well is to get an understanding of the interruption-impact relationship. Interruptions not only take up time when they occur but also cause additional time to go back and repair the train of thought. This delayed effect of interruptions makes it sometimes useful to simply not answer anything at all questioned while being locked down in a concentration period. Only free capacity for self-emergent interruptions should have some room as otherwise one may feel shut away abruptly from members of a group which may have the additional escape effect on itself or the environment preference for enforced discussions.

Good managers often take steps to reduce the overall number of unimportant interruptions to their subordinates, screening phone calls, and dampening the level of demands upon the time and attention of employees. Also, it may be favorable in some situations to dislocate oneself physically from a typically noisy human work environment. Good tools are also available to tampen the noise level of an environment, like MP3 players with noise-canceling headphones intelligent enough to play calm and soothing music under heavy workload, while suddenly suspending it under more quiet conditions. They are appreciated to undo stressful situations by people with types of auditory organizing problems such as ADHD.

Dealing with distractions. It is almost impossible to do creative work or deep thinking without periods of concentration; small interruptions can frustrate this. Distractions in a work environment can make this concentration difficult to achieve. A person who can achieve high levels of concentration and focus his or her thoughts for several uninterrupted hours has a huge advantage over almost all other people in a business.

Incorporating Mindfulness into Daily Life

The practice of the following 7 suggestions will give you an opportunity to apply your presence of mind to your daily activities. If the practice seems dull, keep at it. When your mindfulness grows stronger, you will have a much richer life. Try to raise your awareness in what you are doing at any time, in any circumstance, anywhere. You and everyone else will be better off for it. Incorporating the power of now into your life will transform it. Remember that the whole world is a fascinating circus because now is the only time there is.

It is one thing to experience the present moment in a retreat environment, but quite another to live in the present moment after leaving the retreat. We are surrounded by the myriad of dramas occurring around us, as well as those in our own minds. It may seem a daunting task to prevent these things from pulling us away from the present moment. As one Zen Master said, "It is easy to be enlightened on the mat, but what really counts is to maintain it in life." This chapter is about the process of incorporating mindfulness into each moment of our lives.

Mindful Eating

If you've ever tried to lose weight, even 5 pounds, you may have brought mindful eating into your life. Figuring out what real hunger feels like, when to stop until the next meal, what hunger pangs really are... is all at the base of mindful eating. Only when you can connect to hunger, identify the psychological triggers that send you to the inside of a pack of double-stuffed Oreo cookies feeling like an automatic pilot, or disconnected from the act of gratifying the urge to eat with the senses, does it stand a chance of making a contribution to your health. Now I'm not going to guarantee that you'll like mindful eating any better than deep belly-hungry. And nobody said it would be easy to carry at all times, even if you understood its benefits. Before it becomes a habit, which happens with repetitive attempts, repetition and attention are what make it work. Like getting to Carnegie Hall, it requires practice. Your surroundings could be distracting, and you could be busy.

Although there are probably innumerable benefits to mindless eating, as far as having a remedy (paying attention to our eating), it often results in poor digestion, poor health, overweight, and psychological dissatisfaction.

Try and imagine eating a meal without being conscious of it. Surprisingly, it can happen. Have you ever eaten a bag of popcorn during a 2-hour movie and reached the bottom of the bag with crumbs still clinging to your fingers? You weren't really conscious of every bite, were you? How did that popcorn taste? What did it feel like in your mouth when chewed? Tasting each individual kernel and being fully attentive to each bite you take is what we call mindful eating.

CHAPTER 7

The Neuroscience of Mindfulness

Mindfulness is never more relevant than at the current historical time, as it has been found to be helpful in the management of clinical symptoms of mood disorders, the stress of chronic illness, and the emotions of distress that often accompany stressful work situations. Consequently, it begs the question, "How does it actually work?" Is mindfulness beneficial to mental and physical health and worthy of exploration in scientific studies? The answer is surely yes as we do not need to appeal to eastern mysticism, the teachings of a prophet, or wishful thinking to draw this conclusion, but to solid scientific investigation that has evidenced that these claims are probably correct. A more appropriate question, therefore, would be, "What is the science of mindfulness?" which is the aim of this chapter.

Scientific interest in mindfulness began to grow as a consequence of studies like these and many others that similarly suggested an association between mindfulness and psychological health. To some extent, interest was also driven by the emergence of better scientific methods for observing and analyzing the brain. Modern neuroscience techniques enabled us to study the workings of the healthy brain in living subjects, allowing us to make associations between the mind and the brain in humans for the first time in history. Mindfulness provides a rich subject for investigation, as it is a clearly defined mental process relevant to the everyday life of anyone, and one that can be experienced many thousands of times during the day.

Impact on Brain Function

Presence is a state of inner spaciousness that is completely fresh. With practice, the experience of spaciousness that is conjured up by being unconditionally present will become the natural state. Thoughts may take you on wild adventures now and then, regardless of your present level of development, but you will now have a major contrast to your own thoughts that will prevent the experiences that your thoughts can create. They are only this powerful when they are unconscious. They cannot capture conscious awareness, for awareness is far vaster than the mind. Therefore, presence is pure power. It vanquishes the uninvited thoughts that are trying in vain to invade your consciousness. They will continue to come, but they will always leave again, and you'll always remain. So let them work on you for as long as they'd like. In the end, you will lose nothing through the process, beyond what needs to be lost.

Presence Itself Is Pure Power

The following are some of the main findings that can help you and revolutionize your life as you begin to apply them. You don't have to believe them. In fact, it is easier if you don't. Try them out.

CHAPTER 8

Mindfulness in Different Cultures and Traditions

In Sufism, the mystical dimension of Islam, the word for mindfulness is heedfulness. The nature of the heedfulness and presence is the same in Sufism as in Buddhism. In Chinese Buddhism, "situ" is the word for mindfulness. In Chinese Zen or Chan, sometimes another word is used, which is translated as suchness or thusness. In Iran, a traditionally Islamic country but also with a strong Sufi tradition, I met many people who certainly I did not consider to be spiritually advanced, but who lived in a state of continuous present-moment awareness grouped under the idea of heedfulness. The state they lived in was exactly the same as that taught by the Eastern spiritual teachings. In Japan and Korea, the word for mindfulness is best translated as presence of mind. In the Hindu tradition, the practice of the presence was pioneered by Krishnamurti, who coined this best-ever word for mindfulness. Now, it has crept into the English language, so that we can say, quite correctly, that Krishnamurti spoke of mindfulness, even though the Hindu sacred languages do not have a commonly used word for it. Advice is given to help enable spiritual development in the word the practitioner uses, such as attending.

The concept of mindfulness is not culture-bound. None of these traditions says you need to use the word mindfulness. The important thing is the quality of the awareness itself. Nevertheless, in Oriental languages there are words that are commonly used to translate the English word mindfulness. Thus, we have "sati" in Pali, the language of the earliest Buddhist scriptures, which is usually translated as mindfulness. Sati also means remembering. The essence of mindfulness is a certain presence of mind that is not thinking but is aware of the quality of experience in the here and now.

Buddhist Perspectives on Mindfulness

According to Buddhologist Tadeusz Skorupski, the term sati, although translated nowadays as "mindfulness," should not be understood as "memory" or "recollection," but as the act of bringing back to present mental content, instructions, or one's own tasks and duties, or as the case might be, the immediately present mind's own sensations, states, or qualities.

Mindfulness (Pali: sati) was and is of great importance in Buddhism, although "mindfulness" as a modern concept is generally not considered to be of purely Buddhist origin. In the Satipatthana Sutta, the Buddha identifies four foundations for establishing the practice of mindfulness, to be applied in observing the body, sensations, mental states, and mental objects. Mindfulness interacts with the process of contemplation to reach insight. The conjunction of mindfulness and clear comprehension (sati-sampajañña) is central to the specification of the Eighth. In traditional Buddhist practice, samadhi is developed through the practice of different meditation objects, and this combined with vipassana results in insight. However, the result is a natural outgrowth of long training. Without experience in Buddhist meditation, a reading of the book "The Power of Now" might give rise to some, but probably not all, of the same states.

CHAPTER 9

The Intersection of Mindfulness and Psychology

There are three core components to this learned non-viewing: intention, attention, and attitude. It is how these three components interact together that makes this form of paying attention unique, despite how simple they sound. Together, they create a moment-to-moment consciousness of our daily lives that affects our thoughts and emotions and their meaning. At this intersection of mindfulness and psychology, we find that mindfulness offers a way of meeting and befriending the challenges of our lives that are common to all humans. It introduces a way of being that can promote meaning and purpose.

The term "mindfulness" is increasingly popular and is used in a variety of ways. Dialectical Behavior Therapy, Acceptance and Commitment Therapy, and other evidence-based psychological treatments include mindfulness. These treatments may be helpful to people with depression, anxiety, or other distress. However, mindfulness itself is actually non-view, a specific way of paying attention in the present moment that we all have the potential to develop. Khème considers meditation to be the practice of repetition, turning the mind's attention away from the activity of habit. The result of this practice, deliberately paying attention to the present moment over time, seems to include personal growth, also known as wisdom.

Applications in Therapy

Actually, present-centered awareness enables the person to make the connection that the campaigning voice in their head, probably from past pain, is not real and not from their own voice, but takes away the real reality of today. EMDR is a powerful therapy in providing a modus operandi in reaching healing of discomfort quickly and without much pain. This modern technique is based on how the present moment can be controlled in a way that makes the personal awareness of the situation no longer frightening. The need to focus on the traumatic or painful area in thought process must happen, and in this process, as the present is both felt and seen, formations based on past difficulties can then disappear. The opportunity to complete a final resonance is achieved and comprehended. Time-based trauma, however, calls for time-focus changes, for these experiences are over and once able to see through the present and into the now, they are able to experience the real feeling of the moment itself and hence reduce the painful torment.

In therapy and counseling, it is important to help clients stay focused in the present moment to avoid adopting past emotional influences, future worries, and provide a constant threat of reducing self-awareness on the emotional difficulties. The present moment awareness technique has been found to be very successful with some cases of people who are autistic or experiencing the emptiness of anhedonia, helping to create a sense of joy and awe, and strengthening a sense of self. These people, who experience uncontrolled negative reactions to the activities and feelings of life, can use the power of present awareness to re-experience the pleasures and range of experiences that are expected of life.

CHAPTER 10

Mindfulness in the Workplace

The majority of people can only extract a fraction of what is available within them. Distractions never allow us to give anything our full attention. We expend energy on worrying whether we are doing the right thing rather than going with the 'flow'. Instead of taking constant pleasure in our activities, we dwell either on the past or the future, which leads to stress. To work without stress is to give your fullest attention to each activity as you're performing it, whether the activity itself is your primary interest or not. This means mindfulness. It also means detachment from the focus on goals or rewards. The slower and more focused your actions, the more efficient and satisfying they become.

Mindfulness in the workplace should serve the primary purpose of utmost efficiency without any form of stress. Stress can only be existent when you don't like what you're doing. When you're complacent and just play at your work, stress will threaten your spirit and immune system. Struggle will disappear when you embrace your real nature of stress-free and creative beings in every moment of your life, 24 hours a day. Work can be a great opportunity to practice mindfulness. The more interested you are in any aspect of your work, the more efficient, creative, and satisfied you will become.

Improving Focus and Productivity

By focusing on the present moment instead of wrestling with the unplanned future or rehashing the unchangeable past, the now becomes our primary area of concentration. In this way, by concentrating on the "one" thing we are doing, we greatly increase the chances of excellent performance, avoiding the rut of mediocrity. Provided, of course, that the "one" thing chosen is a positive, productive one. The mind, in focusing on the now, becomes the attentive mind, earmarked by being at place, at the right time, doing what needs to be done, and focusing on those one things that are important for overall success.

The activities of mind, particularly the thoughts of the untrained mind, can contribute to clutter in thinking. Indeed, unwanted mental clutter can be a major block to concentration, productivity, and effectiveness. Simply stated, mental clutter consists of all nonproductive or unproductive activities stemming from having too much to do or think in too little time. The end result is that the effective and efficient operation of the executive mechanism (mind) is compromised, indeed paralyzed.

CHAPTER 11

Mindfulness for Children and Adolescents

When the mother, full of mindfulness, hears the baby crying, she wakes up her wisdom, which then takes the baby in its arms. Mother and child need each other in order to overcome the difficulties. The mother recognizes the crying ("I am suffering, I am suffering...") and both mother and child become calmer. They calm down, sitting still with the suffering—together, the mother holding the baby close. Mindfulness is the mother; the baby is the crying, the suffering. When the energy of mindfulness is born and touches suffering, it is transformed. Mindfulness is there to take care of the suffering, to recognize it. Mindfulness recognizes, embraces, and tenderly holds the crying and soothing thought, "My dear, I am here. I will take care of you." Together, through the united efforts of the mother's mindfulness and the baby's cry, the energy of mindfulness is created from which transformation occurs.

As soon as you bring in the awareness "This is suffering," the energy of mindfulness begins to take care of the suffering. Mindfulness has the energy of concentration and recognizes the suffering, just as a mother recognizes the crying of her baby. My child, whether in the womb, or just born, or a grown-up, if you cry, if you suffer, I am here. I will sit down and find out why. I want you to recognize mindfulness like a mother. "My dear, I have returned to recognize the presence of the crying of my suffering in order to recognize and transform it." The suffering will transform itself from a baby who cried a lot in the womb, bringing his or her suffering to the mother's attention, into a baby who continues to cry, but now with less and less suffering.

Benefits in Education

In the discipline of self-awareness, mindfulness encourages being in the now. Mindfulness exercises focus attention on breathing, listening, seeing, tasting, smelling, and movement. When my students practice mindful walking, they enjoy walking for the present, for no other reason but to experience the sensations of moving each bone and muscle (in a sequential process) on their journey around campus. If the session is done with good humor, students walk up to ten or twenty times around a designated space, purposely bumping into fellow students. Then, they laugh at how carefully others walk to avoid being bumped! Participants tell me they are aware of their honest walking behavior but not of their motivation—or they feign attempting to convince me they purposely bumped into others to bring them to a state of mindfulness!

Children and young adults are ripe to explore the benefits of living in the present moment. Instinctively, we know the benefits of living in the present moment: enriched relationships, creativity, curiosity, focus, and deepened learning. However, the demands of fast-paced, media-driven daily life preclude us from focusing on the here and now. The solution to this issue lies in the process-oriented, experiential, qualitative methods of mindfulness, creativity, and curiosity. How do these methods foster living in the present moment? How can educators help students learn these time-honored, human qualities? What are the human benefits to learning and retaining these qualities—and living in the present moment?

CHAPTER 12

The Role of Mindfulness in Health and Wellness

Finally, mindfulness fosters changes in belief systems that may allow people to better navigate and respond to suffering, either directly or indirectly, and that can help one develop improved coping skills. Examples of later changes in beliefs include desiring personal growth, responsibility in diet and exercise behavior, poignancy or woke values, and beliefs that help to spark imaginative growth in one's thinking. Mindfulness reduces attachment to the world of appearance, regulating thoughts to maintain positivity.

Third, mindfulness interventions appear to enhance the capacity for change, for reevaluation of life patterns, for the cultivation of increased awareness and attentiveness to physical, emotional, spiritual, and relational well-being, and for bringing into sharper focus one's unique insights about life and their own spiritual and existential values. Although research subjects respond more favorably to mindfulness that aligns with their own values, secular counterparts also experience benefits.

First, mindfulness enhances the ability to attend to sensations and becomes "an alternative to unconscious acting out and psychological denial." Mindfulness, compassion, self-compassion, and self-regulation comprise important processes by which mindfulness and related interventions work their improvements. Second, enhanced mindfulness and well-being emerge with iterative training to cultivate connection with the present moment. Graduates emerge from silent retreats, for example, feeling more satisfied and more connected to the world around them.

Mindfulness and mind-body skills stress attending to the present moment without judgment, an awareness of physical sensations, bodily processes, and one's state of mind. Research has linked these qualities to better health, reduced symptoms during illness, healthier lifestyle choices, improved self-management of chronic conditions such as pain and high blood pressure, better psychological functioning, and improved quality of life. These often significant effects unfold along dimensions of change targeting the essential mind-body connection.

Stress Reduction and Resilience

Balbeer was not some mystical figure distanced from the pressures of modern life. He was Chief Operations Officer for a major chemical company, responsible for twenty-eight factories worldwide, all of which needed to be reorganized. He visited six countries within the space of only fourteen days. He said, "I was always on a twenty-four-hour world schedule," yet Balbeer was able to use mindfulness, as we can, to live a calmer, less judgmental, and more vibrant life.

"A final sense of not to worry means to realize that everything rests on your self; all problems are your own making. It is the most important inscription in my house. I learned it with all my being. Not to worry."

There are two aspects to stress: the situation that you are facing and the way that you respond to the situation, the thoughts that you create inside you. You have little or no control over the second aspect. You have no control over the one constant in your life, an underlying ground that still remains when everything else is in flux, your true nature. This is the key to the Inner Kingdom, the key to the birthright, and the key to the natural meditation that is within. Once you realize that things are the way they are and cannot be changed, you come into a new relationship; you begin to see the world in the truth that it is.

CHAPTER 13

Ethical Considerations in Mindfulness Practice

This decoupling has produced a rather interesting and complex situation in which a technique that is based on an ethic often finds itself inserted in secular situations that seem to demand neutrality. For instance, in the specific case of despite being first proposed as part of the original mindfulness-based cognitive-behavioral treatment, an emphasis on ethical conduct is rarely, if ever, directly mentioned. Where it is mentioned, it is typically only by paying indirect attention to the Buddha and keeping all of his teachings in mind, producing a virtue by association. Conduct is implicit in the need to avoid distracting feelings that could potentially be brought up by attending to bodies of people to whom one had long-term karmic relationships, as this could constitute a breach of the ethical principles of Buddhism.

From the Buddhist perspective, in which mindfulness usurps an important and omnipresent role, its practice is generally nested firmly and directly in a wide array of ethical teachings and moral injunctions. However, on its journey to modern contexts, the practice of mindfulness has occasionally been decoupled from its ethical moorings. Most of mindfulness-based interventions are essentially secular in nature and tend to emphasize what is done for the specific purposes and outcomes of reduced symptomatology and enhanced psychological adjustment and well-being. However, this, for good or ill, also presupposes a certain value neutrality.

Cultural Appropriation

It should be kept in mind, however, that "leadership" is a rigorously guarded institution in all shamanic and meditative cultures, a path attainable by few, a true guru being an epitome of rigorous life-long dedication to an exploring process valued since the time of Upanishads. In the present-day Western context, the considerable confusion and misunderstanding surrounding the idea of cultural diversity can cause one serious problems that may result in erroneous experiences. To put it differently, the potential damage involved in religious and cultural practices lies in disregarding the trans-historical symbolic contexts that give them epistemic force. To all appearances, The Power of Now is more actively received by those people who are already predisposed culturally and keen on revaluating Oriental aspects of spiritual life.

The positive reception of Asian spiritual teachings in recent decades has led to an increasing fascination with what are seen as the exotic virtues of the Eastern lifestyle, including a largely Manichean division between materialistic Western civilization with its mindless consumerism and the more exemplary Eastern way of life with its caring community and satisfaction derived from the quality of mind and consciousness. As a result, many Westerners nowadays regard Eastern spiritual practices as something akin to newfound "inner wealth," self-soothing instruments that perfectly complement their affluent lifestyle and reinforce the notion that despite their material wealth, they are, in fact, quite exchanging the material power of their wealth to acquire "true happiness," which they then gloat over. In this respect, spiritual teachings, including The Power of Now, are thought to encourage the formation of a unity that is believed to empower members of all walks of life, acting to establish a readiness for social integration.

CHAPTER 14

The Future of Mindfulness Research and Application

With such wealth of empirical and anecdotal evidence, it is expected that the popularity of mindfulness in Western countries will soar in the near future, creating a third wave of contemplative practices. The first wave was generated by India's iatrogenic invasion; England's colonialist Asianists and academics birthed the second wave; and the third wave is made possible due to the telecommunication, low cost of travel, and the transdisciplinary integration of diverse scientific disciplines that have taken form since the 1950s. The implications to fields like anthropology, philosophy, neuroscience, psychology, and psychiatry are immense as this new influx of contemplative-minded individuals seed these fields with novel tourist perspectives from a journey to the unknown, arising compass-like from their own tenements. Tangentially, it is difficult to predict what social changes may manifest as mindfulness and meditation grow in popularity and its positive life-changing effects diffuse through society. A decrease in consumption of status-affirming possessions and passive forms of entertainment, along with an increase in empathy and healthier lifestyle choices, might be an initial social sign.

During the past 10 to 15 years, there has been an enormous growth in the number of studies that examine the effects of formal mindfulness meditation. Clinical applications for individuals that suffer from chronic pain, recurrent depression, and anxiety disorders have been ascertained. These clinical applications in many instances are based on an 8-week mindfulness-based stress reduction program. Studies have also revealed improved cognitive performance and more flexible emotional responses to stress in undergraduate students following an 8-week training period for mindfulness meditation. More longevity research is needed, yet initial evidence points toward preserved telomere lengths and cellular aging related to mindfulness practice. Moreover, positive testimonials have also come from experienced meditators.

Emerging Trends

It is essential that we make the most of this trend in our research, maintaining sharp perspectives that will lead to transformations in lifestyles.

Interface research should also make it possible for the individual conducting the evaluation work to gain understanding. It is crucial that the research we are doing to develop practical motion input techniques remain useful and stimulating. Debate regarding usage contexts has finally entered the mainstream-marketing varieties of lifestyles have been used to maximize the targets of practical design.

Researchers at work in these areas are moving forward by constantly thinking about the issues of action. They face a number of crucial questions. How should we evaluate the interface problems of these devices, which are now becoming practical for non-experts to use?

The themes of motion and balance are evident in emerging trends in the scenes concentrating on movement devices (VR, AR, and MR) and those on motion input techniques (e.g., touchless interaction). Even with a focus on motion, however, all is not action. In the innovation process, it is crucial to find a quiet corner in which to reconsider.

CHAPTER 15

Conclusion

Work is not the only element of human existence that can be trivialized, if one isn't careful. Love can also be cheapened to the point of meaninglessness. Marriage, often referred to as the most profound of human relationships, has been reduced merely to food, drink, clothing, real estate, procreation, and children. When marriage is stripped of spiritual significance, it becomes just another common dream. It should be remembered that spiritual concerns will be addressed, whether one is open to the prompting of their inner voice or whether the unconscious is left to handle that side of existence as well.

Keep in mind that the idea of living in the now and doing everything in life more fully can be applied to menial labor as well as grand or celebratory events. Whether life is at its zenith of exhilaration or in the depths of drudgery, the power of now can be applied. It would be a grave mistake to consider tedious tasks as obstacles in the way of attaining a level of spirituality. Truthfully, they are indispensable tools in the journey. If your daily manual work does not add up to the amount of spiritual value as the most exalted activities, it is only because the distance between you and the work is too great. That distance is the only thing you have to decrease in order to increase your fulfillment in performing the work.

Key Takeaways and Reflections

In the present moment, we can give ourselves to others, recognizing them for who they are without trying to change them. Holding unconditionally onto the present is what makes up the Essential Individual from which the column tells us we should derive our happiness. And in our effort to become Essential Individuals, it reminds us that we need to start from the bottom. If the vertical and horizontal aspects of our lives are always interconnected and refer to each other, how can we include the present in our daily lives without having to tax our brains with the effort of being present all the time? Kakuzo Okakura's words give us some advice.

By being firmly anchored in the present moment, we can stay calm, free from the suffering caused by future worries and regrets about things that have already happened. By doing this, we can maintain our self-control, making the most of every situation that presents itself to us. Practicing presence keeps us out of the habit of attaching final and unquestionable values to historical situations which, however precious, cannot be changed, and reminds us to be patient. The present moment is fluid. It can be lived in different ways. If we can choose not to rush over it or stop and spend our time repainting a landscape, we can choose how fast we want to travel and to what extent.

www.ingramcontent.com/pod-product-compliance
Lightning Source LLC
Chambersburg PA
CBHW020134180726
47992CB00023B/3042